Rogue Art Genesis:
Contemplative Reflections through Unconventional Art

Rogue Art Genesis:
Contemplative Reflections through Unconventional Art

Brad Morrow

IdeaWorks, Inc
2016

Copyright © 2016 by Brad Morrow

All rights reserved. This book or any portion thereof may not be reproduced or used in any manner whatsoever without the express written permission of the publisher except for the use of brief quotations in a book review or scholarly journal.

First Printing: 2016

ISBN 978-1-365-16509-2

IdeaWorks, Inc.
3801 S. Allegheny Ave.
Tulsa, OK 74135

Contents

Introduction 1
Chapter 1: Transformed Heart 9
Chapter 2: Baggage Handler 13
Chapter 3: Timid Soul 18
Chapter 4: Red Sphere Through White 21
Chapter 5: Freedom for the Marionette 26
Chapter 6: Birth of a Dream 30
Chapter 7: Obscured View 32
Chapter 8: Insights from a Protozoa 35
Chapter 9: What is Truth? 38
Chapter 10: Unrestrained (Outside the Lines) 41
Chapter 11: Two Souls 44
Chapter 12: The Three Mirrors 52
Conclusion 56

Introduction

Rogue [rōg]: - not obedient, no longer controllable, not answerable, a renegade.

Rogue Art is a unique combination of art and philosophy. It is the union of art that breaks with tradition and philosophy geared towards practical application above metaphysical rhetoric. It is an intersection of art and real life where works of mixed media speak to us in such a way that we are drawn to action to be better versions of ourselves.

Each work of Rogue Art has three aspects:
- The Art
- The Questions
- The Call to Action

The Art

Rogue Art beckons the artist to break with convention. Each piece needs to move beyond what is considered the "status quo" of art. The works tend to break rules as they deviate from the norm. Oftentimes the art invites questions like:

Why does paint have to stay on the canvas?

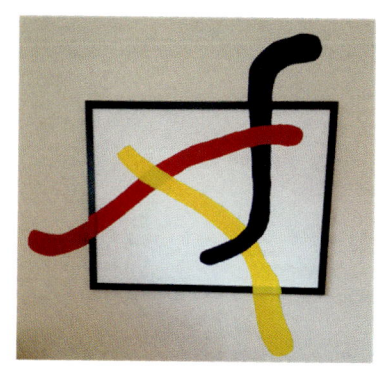

Why are paintings in two dimensions? What could they tell us about ourselves if they were in multiple dimensions?

Rogue Art Genesis

Why does the artist complete the work? What would happen if the viewer had a say in the outcome and in fact was invited to put the final touches on the work?

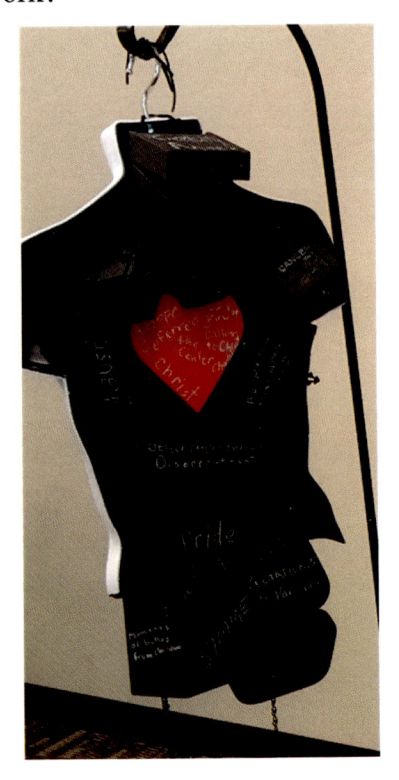

There are a myriad of other questions to ask, a host of rules to break. Rogue Art like a renegade attempts to champion this rule braking behavior in order to draw us to contemplative thoughts about life.

The Questions

Posted next to each work of Rogue Art is a series of questions. These queries call the viewer to look deeply into the work and ask where their life and the art intersect. As the viewer thinks deeply over the questions, the art becomes less of an object to view and more of a mirror of the soul.

We spend a lot of time looking into physical mirrors, but in many cases not near so much time peering into the reflection of the soul. The questions in Rogue Art give people a venue to muse over and reflect on their inner selves. In a sense it gives them the opportunity to slow down and observe what they perhaps have not seen in a very long time - their real selves.

As these questions cause the works to function as mirrors of the inner self, each person sees something different. They may observe aspects of themselves they really like, or perhaps things they would like to improve. Whatever the case, the questions guide the viewer to the final and most important aspect of Rogue Art: the call to action.

The Call to Action

After someone reflects on a work of Rogue Art deeply, they see things about themselves. The call to action is yet another question posted near the work, but this question is more pointed and practical. It basically asks, "Having observed your soul, what will you do now?" Suppose one person observes something in themselves that brings joy. What will they do to spread this joy to others? Perhaps someone else will see something they would like to improve. The call to action invites the question, what practical action will you take to see these improvements come to fruition in your life.

The call is purposefully vague. The individual observer must discover detailed practical actions for themselves. In this way the call does not preach or dictate, but rather beckons the individual as a friend to be a better version of themself. Like the coach of a gold medal winning athlete who continues to encourage so the athlete can win the gold in the next Olympics, so the call to action beckons the viewer to look within and discover how they might live with increased joy and love.

How to View Rogue Art

Too much of a good thing

Rogue Art has many compelling ideas to speak to us. Or perhaps more appropriately said, there are many things to discover about ourselves as we look deeply into the works. As such, if we fully observed every work in a Rogue Art exhibit in one day, it would be too much to take in, too many questions, too many calls to actions in a single setting.

The best way to view a Rogue Art exhibit is to look through all the works briefly and see which one beckons you. To which of the pieces are you drawn. Then pick one or at most two and muse over those deeply. Ask yourself each question. Ponder the queries from several different angles. Consider intently how the art is connected to your real life experience.

Give yourself the freedom to take all the time you need. Take ten minutes, twenty minutes, an hour to soak in everything your thoughts reveal about a single work. There is no rush. When the time is right, come back another day and gaze upon another work deeply.

People of faith, ask God for insight

If you are a person of faith, ask God for enlightenment as you observe the works. Pray that God will guide your imagination and thoughts as you peer into these "mirrors of the soul."

How Did Rogue Art Come to Be

Rogue Art came into existence formally as an art form in July of 2013 with the creation of the first work of Rogue Art, *Birth of a Dream*. However, the actual idea of Rogue Art came to me in the following way. Through the years, many ideas would come to mind not just about art, but inventions, books, illusions and many other categories. These ideas started coming so rapidly that one Christmas I asked my wife for the gift of journals so I could begin writing them down before I forgot them. That year she gave me a large stack of journals. I placed them strategically in every location I might receive an idea: my car, my bedroom, my den, my office, my backpack. I began writing down every idea that came to mind.

In my early fifties the company I worked for offered an early retirement package. Although the package was not enough to support retirement, I was able to take a short sabbatical. During my time off I asked the question, "What will I do with the next 50 years of my life?" I began to collate all the ideas from my journals into categories: art ideas, book ideas, inventions, etc. And I wondered which path I should pursue. Then something wonderful happened!

The Ignatius Spiritual Exercises

I was introduced to a series of prayers and contemplative practices developed by St. Ignatius known as the Ignatian Spiritual Exercises. Through these experiences I was encouraged to ask God to guide my imagination as I considered the scriptures and really all aspects of life during prayer. The most beautiful and amazing thing happened. God answered my prayer and began to make my imagination flourish. Ideas began to pour forth like never before. Almost every day new ideas for art work would come to mind. And unlike the ideas I had in my past, these ideas connected me to the scriptures and led to practical application. There were times when I felt that same burning of the prophet Jeremiah as he spoke of God's word in him, "then there is in my heart as it were a burning fire" (Jeremiah 20:9b World English Bible)

Rogue Art Genesis

It was during this time the idea came to me to add to the art questions and calls to action. I believe this concept of Rogue Art came as inspiration from God in answer to my request to guide my imagination. Guide He did! After a time the church I was attending decided to use Rogue Art as a guide and spiritual exercise through Lent. So the idea came to write week long devotionals for each work of art. These devotionals gave people a framework to contemplate the intersection of life, faith and art in the real world. The devotionals gave them a daily contemplation and encouraged them to create their own works of art. This gave the participants a backdrop for weekly small group meetings where people could share their insights freely.

So in a very real sense Rogue Art was birthed, I believe, in the heart and mind of God. Because He longs for us to use our heart and minds together, He has provided the outlet of Rogue Art as another way to bring us insight and to help us be more fully alive.

Comparison to Other Art Forms

Though I formally created Rogue Art in July of 2013, in a real sense many aspects of Rogue Art have existed since the beginning of time. Anytime an artist through the centuries has created something new and outside the realms of what was considered normal, they were creating Rogue Art. From the first artist to draw on a cave wall to the first impressionist to post-modern works and beyond, artists have been thinking outside the borders of what is allowed for centuries. Some artists, like Kazimir Malevich, the creator of the art form Suprematism, were even ordered to cease and desist by their government.

Though Rogue Art tries to break with traditional forms of art, this should not be viewed as a lack of respect or admiration for the historic forms. Rogue Art is rather a tribute to the masters, who through the ages brought new revelation to humanity through their innovation and creativity. Their historic witness calls us to do the same.

So it is with awe and respect that Rogue Art pays tribute to those great thinkers who brought us light and enlightenment. We do this by following their lead of continuously stepping outside the lines of normal by forcibly bursting through the walls of the status quo. And if we strive hard enough, our hope is to bring even a fraction of the enlightenment brought by those great visionaries of the ages.

How to Use This Book

This book contains the images, questions and calls to action for the first dozen works of Rogue Art created. As stated earlier, it is unwise to try and fully absorb all the insights from all the works in one sitting. This book allows you to take them in over time. Consider spending a few minutes each day for a full week with a single work. Come back to the same work each day and muse over the questions deeply. Ponder the call to action. Reflect on how you are doing as you try to apply the insights you glean.

You may want to consider gathering a small group of friends for a weekly meeting to look at the same work and share your interpretations and insights with one another. Perhaps you might use the companion devotional guide, *Devotionals for Rogue Art Genesis*, as well which provides daily devotions for a week-long look at each of the twelve works.

The important thing is to let this short book provide you with enlightenment for months rather than days. There is no rush; let the works soak in and be like a healing salve and a joyful encouragement to your soul.

Conclusion

Rogue Art reaffirms my conviction that art is emotion. Art in all its forms is emotion. From a comedy monologue to the ballet, from slam poetry to oil on canvas, art makes us feel. And the more it makes us feel, the more fully alive we become.

It is my hope that as you peer deeply into the works in this book and muse intently over the questions and calls to action, you will feel the art at work within you. As you look into these mirrors of the soul, they will bring light and enlightenment. And may you have a genuine sense of being more fully alive as a result of your engagement with these works.

Enjoy the journey into Rogue Art!

Chapter 1: Transformed Heart

I will also give you a new heart, and I will put a new spirit within you; and I will take away the stony heart out of your flesh, and I will give you a heart of flesh.

Ezekiel 36:26 (World English Bible)

Rogue Art Genesis

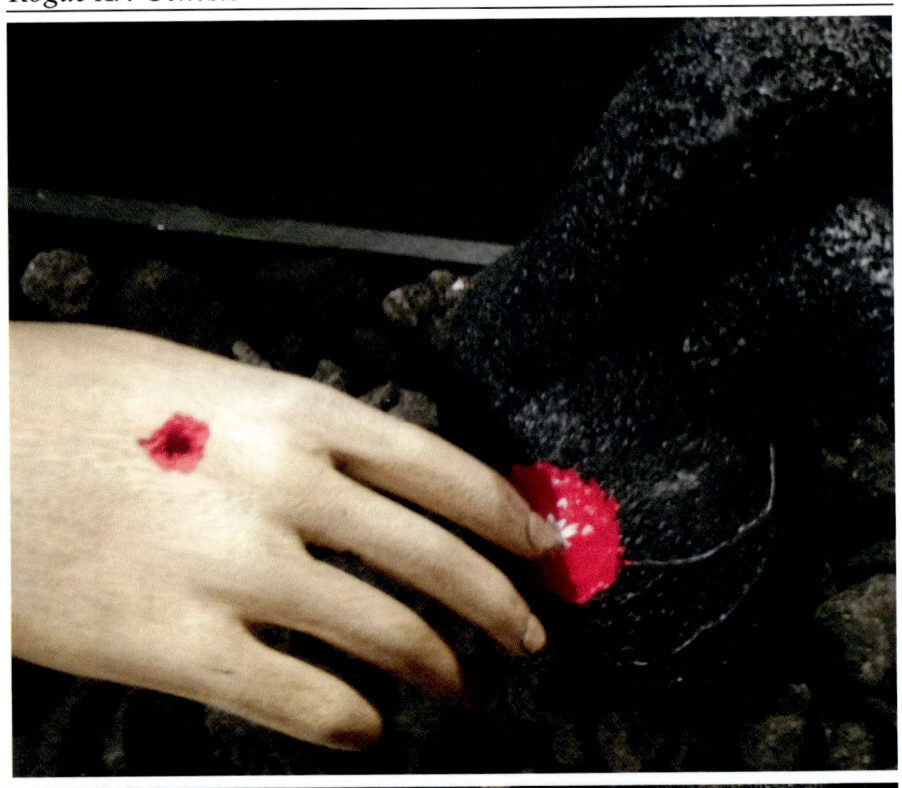

Consider the heart of stone before you and the wounded hand that touches it. At the point of first contact, light touches the heart and it begins to change to a heart of flesh.

Questions to Consider

This work is a snapshot in time. At the moment the snapshot was taken, how long had the hand been touching the heart?

Why is the hand wounded? Who inflicted this wound?

Do you think it is possible to have a partially transformed heart? If so, what would that look like in the real world?

What is the condition of your heart? Is it where you want it to be? If not, how might you seek the Lord for transformation?

Call to Action

In answer to the last question, did you sense you have been living with a transformed heart, at least in part? If so, take a moment to thank God for His healing touch. Consider the great cost He paid to bring about your transformation.

In answer to the last question, did you sense there were things about your heart you would like transformed? Did you think of ways you could seek transformation? If so, when will you follow through with that plan? Will you take it from an abstract idea to practical action?

Final Thoughts

Therefore if anyone is in Christ, he is a new creation. The old things have passed away. Behold, all things have become new.

2 Cor. 5:17 (World English Bible)

Reflections on the wound written 300 years before crucifixion was invented:

> Surely he has borne our sickness,
>   and carried our suffering;
> yet we considered him plagued,
>   struck by God, and afflicted.
> But he was pierced for our transgressions.
>   He was crushed for our iniquities.
> The punishment that brought our peace was on him;
>   and by his wounds we are healed.
> All we like sheep have gone astray.
>   Everyone has turned to his own way;
>   and Yahweh has laid on him the iniquity of us all.

Isaiah 53:4-6 (World English Bible)

Chapter 2: Baggage Handler

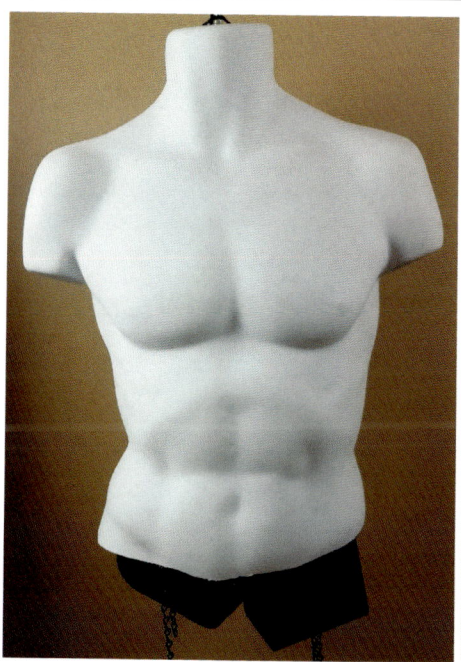

For my yoke is easy, and my burden is light.
                    Matthew 11:30 (World English Bible)

Consider the work above. From the outside he looks like a fine specimen of a man. But from the inside we have a unique glimpse into his soul and we see he is carrying a lot of baggage. Can you step into this man's pain? Can you feel the weight of the burdens he carries hidden within?

Rogue Art Genesis

Brad Morrow

Help Finish the Work

In a rogue art exhibit the baggage in this piece is labeled by the viewers. They are asked to consider what baggage this soul might be carrying and then write the name of the baggage on one of the boxes using chalk. Though you are not at an exhibit, take a moment to think about what baggage this soul might be carrying. What name would you give this baggage? If you had chalk in hand and were near the work what name would you write on one or more of the bags?

Questions to Consider

Did these bags come to the soul all at once or gradually over time?

At what point did this soul stop releasing the weight of burdens encountered? What caused him to linger with his burdens instead of releasing them?

Was it a major life event or a thousand subtle events that left him burdened?

Does he realize he is carrying such burdens? If so, does he really know why or how he ended up carrying them?

When you named one of the bags, why did you select that name? Is it something you carry with you? Is it something you sense in someone else?

How can we gain freedom from carrying the weight of such burdens?

We tend to use the metaphor of carrying baggage in a negative context. However, is there positive baggage? Are there things we carry with us that can make us wiser, or make us more empathetic or help us to love more fully?

Call to Action

We all have emotional pain in our history. We can let it be a cruel taskmaster; a constant reminder of our anguish or we can allow it to make us more fully human; to know the depths so we can arise to empathize and be a better agent of healing.

Trusting in the Lord's grace and power, what action will you take to drop some baggage you carry or assist a friend in freeing them from a burden?

Final Thoughts

Blessed be the Lord, who daily bears our burdens,
   even the God who is our salvation.
>Psalms 68:19 (World English Bible)

Bear one another's burdens, and so fulfill the law of Christ.
>Galatians 6:2 (World English Bible)

Chapter 3: Timid Soul

I came that they may have life, and may have it abundantly.
                                John 10:10b, (World English Bible)

Consider the canvas in front of you. This canvas has been painting himself for many years. He has numerous colors to choose from. He has a whole canvas to paint, yet he limits himself to a single color and to only a small portion of canvas. For years and years he has done this, painting paint upon paint, until he forms a thick, bland hill, never venturing out, never experiencing or expressing the full range and depth of his potential.

Questions to Consider

Why do you think the canvas limits his work to only one small area?

Why does he use only one color when so many are available to him?

Is there anyone keeping him from using the full canvas and multiple colors? Or is his behavior self-imposed?

Call to Action

Are there people you know who have limited their life experience out of fear or concern for risks? How can you assist them to add color and texture to their lives?

Are there areas of the canvas of your life that have yet to be painted? Colors you have yet to use? Can you name these areas? What will you do about this?

Is God calling you to something new? What will you do in response to his calling?

Final Thoughts

"It is not the critic who counts; not the man who points out how the strong man stumbles, or where the doer of deeds could have done them better. The credit belongs to the man who is actually in the arena, whose face is marred by dust and sweat and blood; who strives valiantly; who errs, who comes short again and again, because there is no effort without error and shortcoming; but who does actually strive to do the deeds; who knows great enthusiasms, the great devotions; who spends himself in a worthy cause; who at the best knows in the end the triumph of high achievement, and who at the worst, if he fails, at least fails while daring greatly, so that his place shall never be with those cold and timid souls who neither know victory nor defeat."

Theodore Roosevelt

A Rogue Art Blessing

May you love radically, serve valiantly, and worship with unrestrained passion, free from the fear of the perceptions of others.

May the energizing joy of a noble pursuit overwhelm any anxiety in the path of that pursuit.

May you experience the full gamut of human emotion granting you an authentic awareness that you are fully alive.

May your canvas be vibrant and overflowing with a myriad of colors that brings light, hope and meaning to you and to all those around you.

Chapter 4: Red Sphere Through White

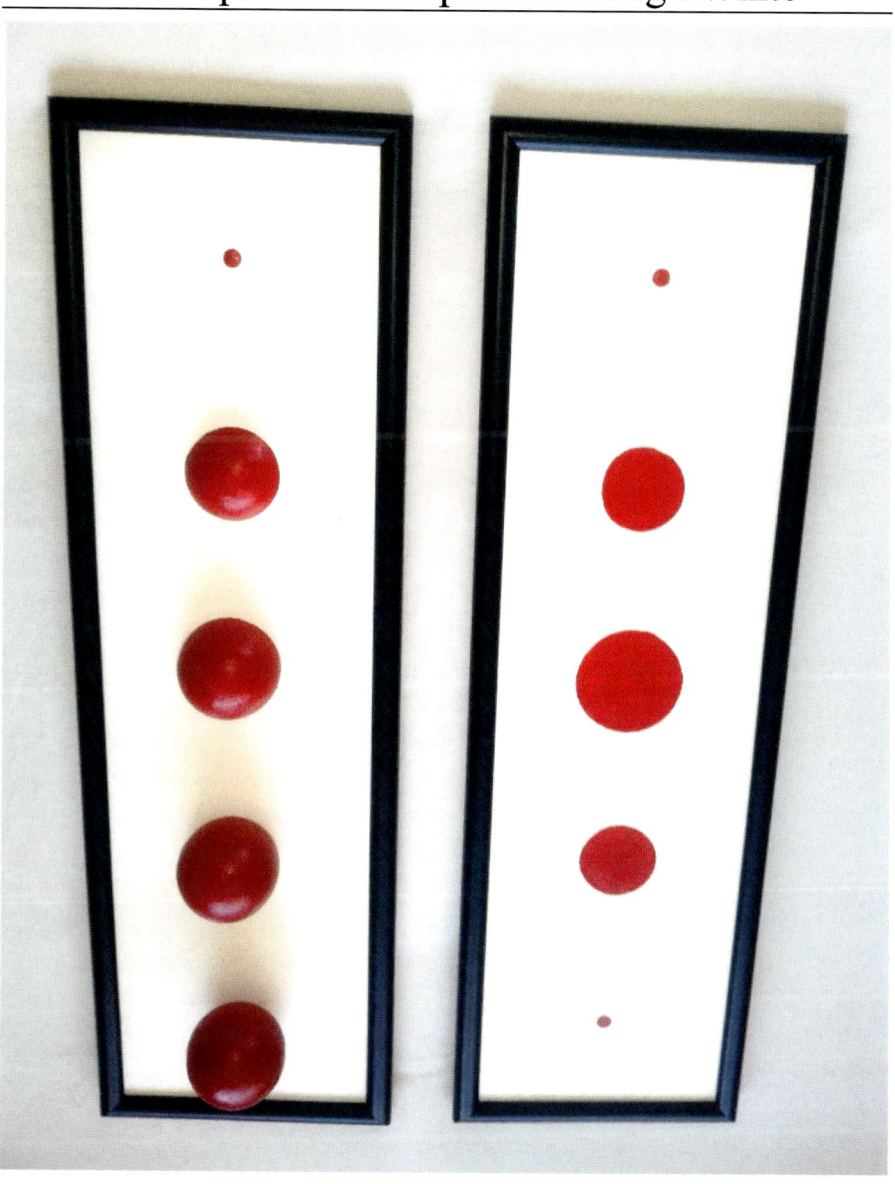

Their eyes were opened, and they recognized him
                        Luke 24:31 (World English Bible)

Rogue Art Genesis

This work is intended to honor two great thinkers:
    Kazimir Malevich – the creator of the art form Supermatism
    Edwin A. Abbot – author of <u>Flatland</u>

The goal of this work is to call us to consider how it is we limit our thinking and to expand our comfort level with mystery and the unknown.

Kazimir Malevich was an artist in the early 1900s. In the decade of 1910 he began communicating the fundamental aspects of Supermatism and created the works *Black Square* and *Red Square (Painterly Realism of a Peasant Woman in Two Dimensions)*. Living in Russia in the late 1920's, many of his works were confiscated, and he was banned from creating similar works as a result of Stalin's stand against abstract forms.

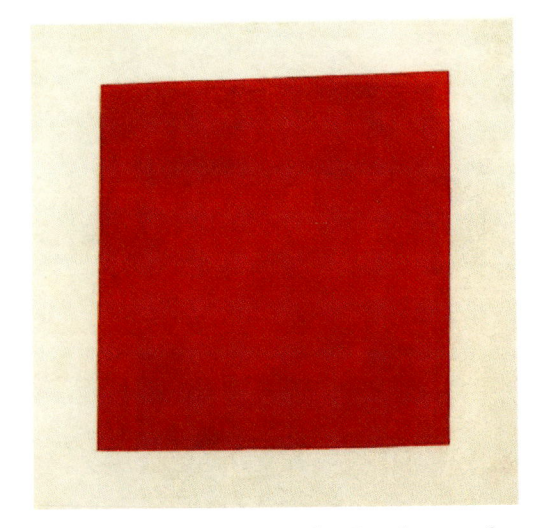

Kazimir Malevich

Red Square (Painterly Realism of a Peasant Woman in Two Dimensions)

Brad Morrow

Edwin A. Abbot was a theologian, English schoolmaster and author of several books. In 1884 he wrote *Flatland, a Romance of Many Dimensions*, the story of a square living in a two dimensional world who is visited by a sphere. In the novel the square suggests to the sphere that perhaps there are other dimensions beyond their ability to perceive; perhaps a fourth, fifth, sixth, etc. Later the square is placed in prison in the two dimensional world for trying to convince people of the existence of three dimensions.

Edwin A. Abbot

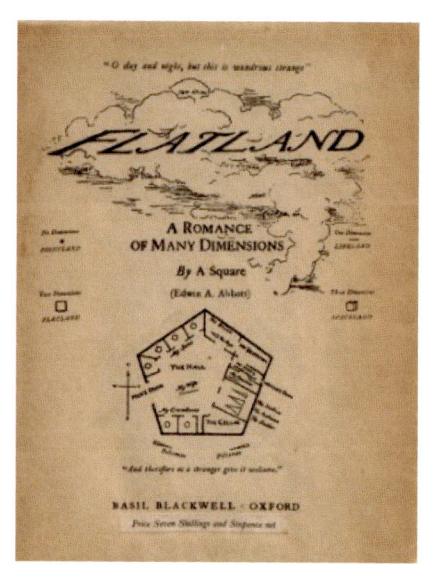

Flatland, a Romance of Many Dimensions

The work *Red Sphere Through White* (on page 21) pays tribute to Malevich's ground-breaking move towards new ways of thinking by moving the notion of shapes on canvas to a third dimension. The piece on the left with the red sphere passing through the canvas, depicts how this work appears in a three dimensional world. The work on the right is the same piece as perceived in a two dimensional world.

Questions to Consider

Envision yourself in the world of Flatland.

How does the Flatlanders' ability to see only in 2 dimensions limit their ability to understand the way things really are?

Is there any advantage for them to only see in 2 dimensions?

Do you think they are worried about their limited ability?

Now consider this:

Though we live in a three dimensional world, our scientists and mathematicians have discovered the existence of at least 10 dimensions in the physical universe. This raises the question: Are there more dimensions beyond what we have discovered? With this in mind, ask yourself:

How does our limited ability to see in only 3 dimensions affect our ability to understand the way things really are?

How does our limited view affect our ability to see God the way He really is? Can we properly and fully comprehend the infinite God, creator of all dimensions?

Call to Action

As 3D humans we have many questions beyond our ability to understand. Allow yourself a greater comfort level with mystery and the currently unexplainable. Give yourself freedom to move from angst to awe, from doubt to determination in an earnest pursuit of truth. Because we have yet to perceive the answers to our questions does not mean the answers do not exist.

Brad Morrow

What questions do you have that currently evade answers? How might you seek answers to these? While in pursuit of answers, how might you gain a greater comfort level with mystery and the currently unexplained? What practical action will you take this week to pursue answers? What practical action will you take this week to pursue embracing mystery?

Final Thoughts

For now we see in a mirror, dimly, but then face to face. Now I know in part, but then I will know fully, even as I was also fully known.

1 Corinthians 13:12 (World English Bible)

Chapter 5: Freedom for the Marionette

If therefore the Son makes you free, you will be free indeed.
John 8:36 (World English Bible)

As you observe this work, visualize the marionette as representative of all humanity as well as of each of us individually.

Brad Morrow

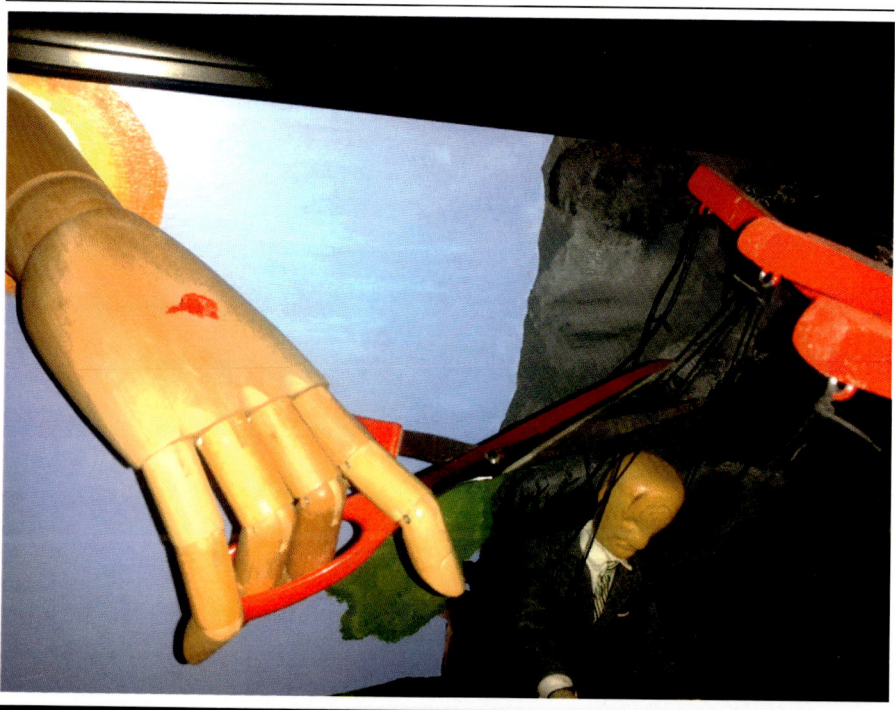

Questions to Consider

Do you think the man is aware of the strings and the forces that are manipulating him?

Do you think the man started out this way, manipulated by the skeleton hand?

The wounded hand is poised to cut the strings, but He is not doing anything yet. Why not? What's He waiting for?

The scissors are poised around one string. When the hand cuts with the scissors, will He cut just the one string or all?

When the marionette is free from the manipulating control of the strings, will he live as a free man? Or has he grown so accustomed to the constant, invisible pull of the strings that he will grope for bondage?

Call to Action

Picture in your mind the movie of the life of the marionette. See his birth in the delivery room coming out with strings attached. As he grows he is on the playground with other children all with strings attached. He starts working; strings attached. He retires and eventually dies. If you were to write the movie of the marionette, at what point would he experience freedom from the strings?

Place yourself as the main character in the movie you just visualized.
- Where are you in this movie?
- Are you free?
- Have you been free, yet the familiarity of the strings has you living as though you are not?
- Are you living in partial freedom?

If you are living in any condition other than complete freedom, what will you do about this?

Final Thoughts

The Spirit of the Lord is on me,
   because he has anointed me to preach good news to the poor.
He has sent me to heal the broken hearted,
   to proclaim release to the captives,
   recovering of sight to the blind,
   to deliver those who are crushed,
           Luke 4:18 (World English Bible),
           Jesus reading from the prophet Isaiah about himself

You will know the truth, and the truth will make you free.
       John 8:32 (World English Bible)

Stand firm therefore in the liberty by which Christ has made us free, and don't be entangled again with a yoke of bondage.
       Galatians 5:1 (World English Bible)

Chapter 6: Birth of a Dream

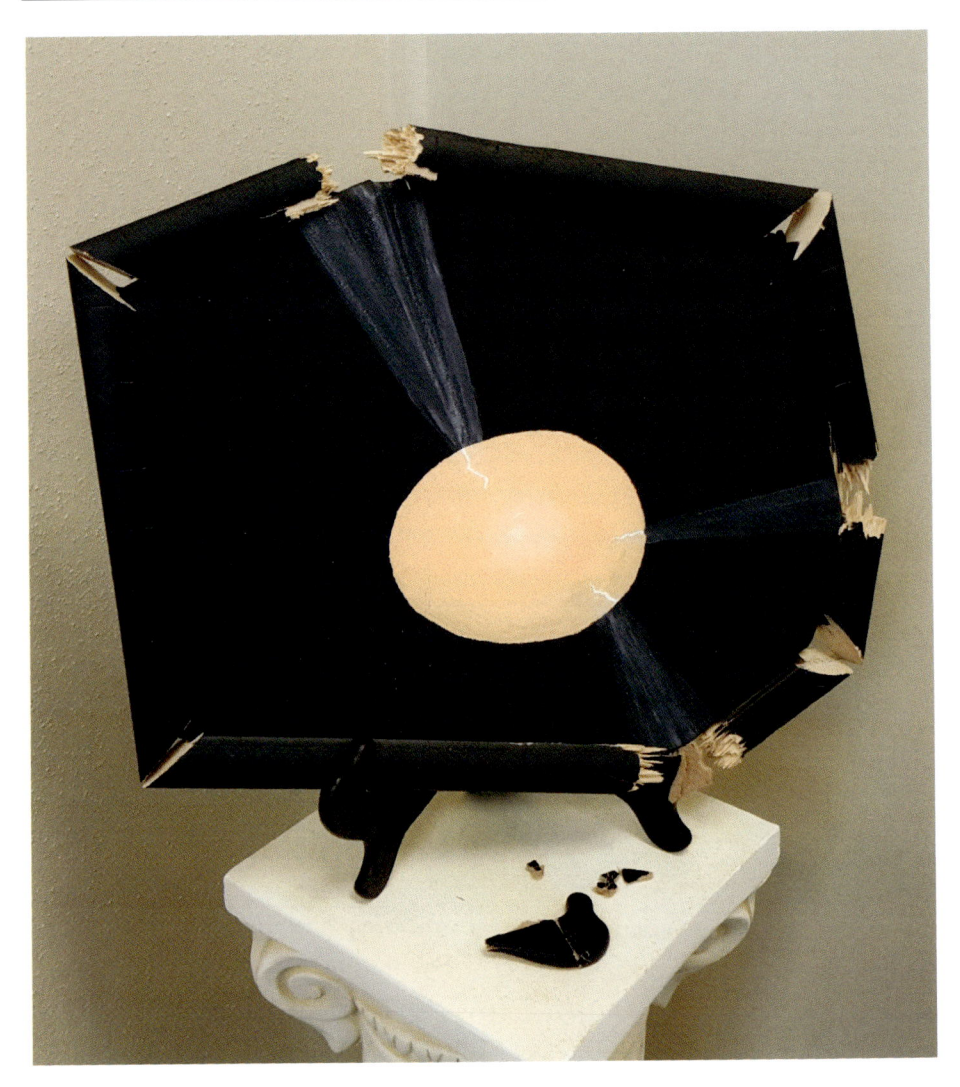

Trust in Yahweh with all your heart,
   and don't lean on your own understanding.
In all your ways acknowledge him,
   and he will make your paths straight.
               Proverbs 3:5, 6 (World English Bible)

Consider before you the hatching egg filled with light. Visualize the light yearning to break out as a dream. Let the frame represent those things that keep us from our dreams:
- Self-doubt
- The opinions of others
- The constant nagging pull of the status quo to keep us unchanged

Questions to Consider

Do you have a dream that is waiting to hatch? What is your dream?

What is keeping you from giving birth to your dream?

When God created you, what did He hope and dream for you?

How has God gifted you? Does He have a plan for you to use those gifts?

Are you using the gifts God has given you?

Are you trusting in the resurrection power that frees and transforms in order to live into the dream and vision God has planned for you? Are there times when you are trusting only in your own strength?

Call to Action

Is God calling you to some form of service you perhaps have not done before? Is He calling you to reignite some dreams from your past? What will you do?

Final Thoughts

"Let your dreams outgrow the shoes of your expectations."
Ryunosuke Satoro

"If you add a little to a little and do this often, soon the little will become great."
Hesiod

Chapter 7: Obscured View

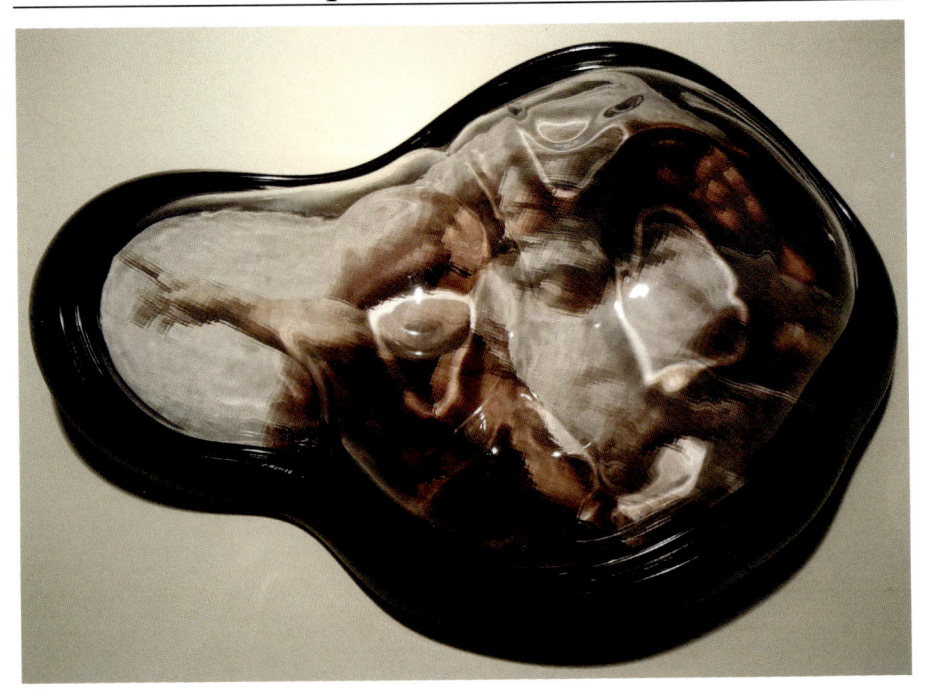

Philip said to him, "Lord, show us the Father, and that will be enough for us."

Jesus said to him, "Have I been with you such a long time, and do you not know me, Philip? He who has seen me has seen the Father. How do you say, 'Show us the Father?'

                                      John 14:8-9 (World English Bible)

Look above and take notice of the image that looks a little like a blurred warped version of Michelangelo's painting of God.

Questions to Consider

Is the image of God hard to see? Why?

This image of God is much smaller than the one on the ceiling of the Sistine Chapel. Why?

What is obscuring the view of God?

What do you suppose caused the image to become warped?

Consider your own view of God. Are there things obscuring that view, keeping you from seeing Him as He truly is?

Does your perspective of God sometimes make Him appear smaller than He really is?

Has culture, history or events in your own life presented you with an incomplete or obscured view of God?

How might you seek God for clearer vision of who He is and what He is really like?

Call to Action

In answer to the last question, "How might you seek God for clearer vision …", how might you turn your answer from the abstract to practical action? What practical steps will you take to pursue God and a clearer vision of Him?

Final Thoughts

"The most dangerous untruths are truths slightly distorted."
Georg C. Lichtenberg

Yahweh says, Don't let the wise man glory in his wisdom, neither let the mighty man glory in his might, don't let the rich man glory in his riches; but let him who glories glory in this, that he has understanding, and knows me, that I am Yahweh who exercises loving kindness, justice, and righteousness, in the earth: for in these things I delight, says Yahweh.
Jeremiah 9:23-24 (World English Bible)

Chapter 8: Insights from a Protozoa

Rogue Art Genesis

Standing still, Jesus commanded him to be brought to him. When he had come near, he asked him, "What do you want me to do?"

He said, "Lord, that I may see again."

Jesus said to him, "Receive your sight. Your faith has healed you."

Immediately he received his sight, and followed him, glorifying God. All the people, when they saw it, praised God.
Luke 18:40-43 (World English Bible)

Consider the conversation between the two protozoa.

Questions to Consider

What are you hesitant to believe in simply because the current ability of your eyes doesn't allow you to perceive it?

Other than your eyes, what "sight" do you possess?

How do we observe the invisible in this world? How do we improve our vision of the unseen?

Call to Action

How will you seek the Lord and what will you do to improve your spiritual "sight" into those things which your vision does not currently allow you to see clearly? Are you comfortable saying to Jesus, "Lord, I want to see" and if so, how might He respond?

Final Thoughts

Having eyes, don't you see?

        Jesus Christ, Mark 8:18a (World English Bible)

"There are two ways of spreading light: to be the candle or the mirror that reflects it."

        Edith Wharton

"I live and love in God's peculiar light."

        Michelangelo

"The real voyage of discovery consists of not in seeking new landscapes but in having new eyes."

        Marcel Proust

"One sees great things from the valley, only small things from the peak."

        G. K. Chesterton

Chapter 9: What is Truth?

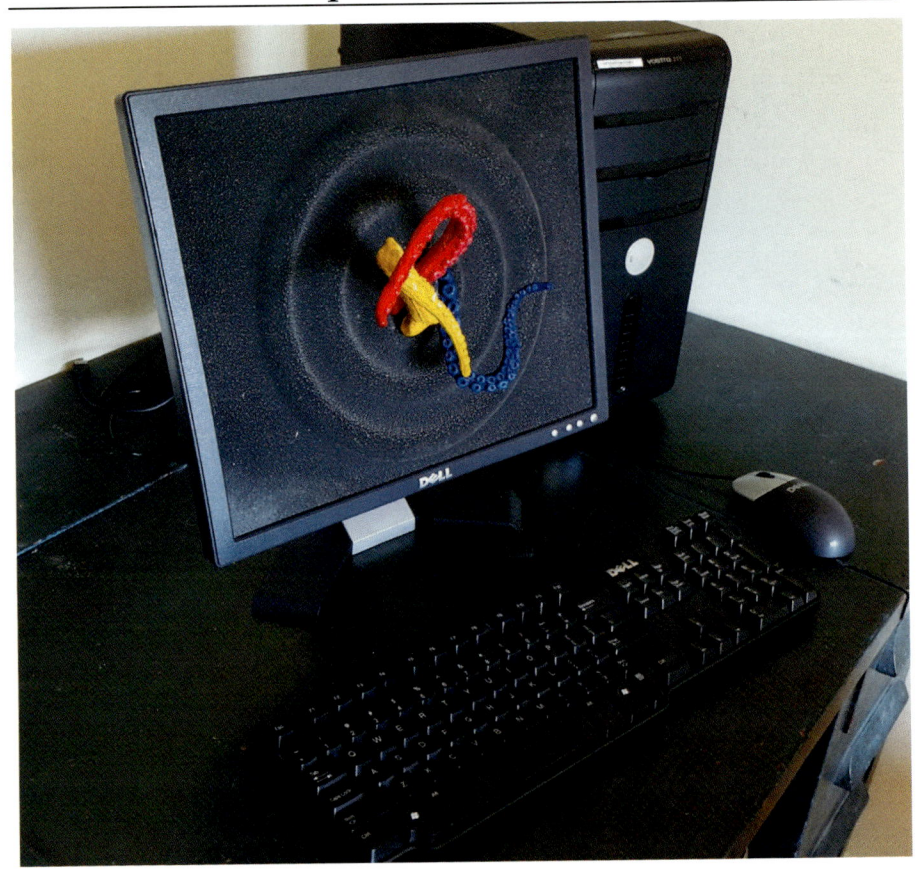

Pilate therefore said to him, "Are you a king then?"

Jesus answered, "You say that I am a king. For this reason I have been born, and for this reason I have come into the world, that I should testify to the truth. Everyone who is of the truth listens to my voice."

Pilate said to him, "What is truth?"
John 18:37-38a (World English Bible)

Brad Morrow

Consider the computer monitor above. Think of it as a metaphor for all sources of information, the internet, the media, etc. Reflect on the squid tentacles as symbolic of the many ways various "truths" thrust themselves upon us. Let the three colors represent different thoughts about what "truth" is, with each color representing a different opinion on truth.

Questions to Ponder

How do you decide what is true with so many options being thrust upon you?

Is it possible we at times embrace something as true out of convenience, accepting what is laid before us because it is easier than laboring to uncover actual truth?

Is it possible you have embraced something as true that is in fact false? How would you find out?

How would you seek real truth?

What is truth?

Call to Action

How can you seek truth more fervently? What practical steps can you take to live in truth? What can you do to insure your outward actions are consistent with what you inwardly hold to be true?

Final Thoughts

You will know the truth, and the truth will make you free.
John 8:32 (World English Bible)

"There are a terrible lot of lies going about the world, and the worst of it is that half of them are true."
Winston S. Churchill

"Art is the lie that enables us to realize the truth."
Pablo Picasso

"There are no facts, only interpretations."
Friedrich Nietzsche

"There are two ways to be fooled. One is to believe what isn't true; the other is to refuse to believe what is true."
Søren Kierkegaard

"Wrong does not cease to be wrong because the majority share in it."
Leo Tolstoy

Chapter 10: Unrestrained (Outside the Lines)

For my thoughts are not your thoughts,
and your ways are not my ways," says Yahweh.
Isaiah 55:8 (World English Bible)

Rogue Art Genesis

For a moment ponder one possible interpretation for the work above:
- The seemingly vague lines of color represent streams of thought.
- The frame represents a border attempting to hold the thoughts at bay. The frame is the well-meaning intentions of polite society to resist change.

Consider these examples of streams of thought from history that encountered resistance. Let the colors represent these and similar thoughts:

- When Dr. King sought to change the thinking of a nation about race.

- When Galileo sought to change the perceptions of our position in the universe.

- When Jesus Christ sought to change the definition of greatness by saying, "But he who is greatest among you will be your servant." Matthew 23:11 (World English Bible)

Questions to Consider

What are some other examples of "streams of thought" you can think of from history?

What are some other examples of "borders to resist change" from history?

What are some examples of "streams of thought" you can think of from your life?

What are some examples of "borders to resist change" which are trying to limit your thoughts from being fully realized?

Call to Action

Based on the streams of thought and borders in your life, what specific action can you take to live in a more unrestrained way? How will you practically carry your streams of thought past the border to fruition so they become a reality?

Examples to kick-start your thinking:

- If you are a scientist or engineer, are you limiting your research or inventions to minor variations of what has been done in the past? Take time to consider your research from a completely different angle and see where it leads you.

- If you are a person of faith, have you limited your belief to more readily fit into the tidy borders of society? How will you cross the border to love more radically and live in more freedom?

Final Thoughts

"The important thing in science is not so much to obtain new facts as to discover new ways of thinking about them."
William Bragg

"Few minds wear out; more rust out."
Christian Nestell Bovee

"A great many people think they are thinking when they are merely rearranging their prejudices."
William James

Chapter 11: Two Souls

Brad Morrow

Rogue Art Genesis

> Rejoice with those who rejoice. Weep with those who weep.
> Romans 12:15 (World English Bible)

> Love your neighbor as yourself.
> Leviticus 19:18b, Matthew 22:39b, Galatians 5:14b
> (World English Bible)

One day, as I considered the concept of Rogue Art, questions came to me:
- Why do paintings hang on the wall?
- Why don't they hang in midair?
- If they did hang in midair, what could they tell us about ourselves and humanity?

As I considered this, the realization came that perhaps paintings on the wall are like us to some degree. They have a portion of themselves they display for all to see. But there is a part that is hidden from view. Perhaps the less seemly part of our soul; sections in our past or our thoughts we do not care to be displayed.

With this in mind, consider these two souls before you. The two paintings represent the perspectives of two souls as they view the exact same scene at the exact same time.

Questions to Consider Regarding the Front

You cannot directly see the scene these souls are looking at; you are only observing it through their eyes. Which soul do you suppose has the more accurate view of reality?

If these two are looking at the exact same thing at the same time, what could cause such a radical difference in their perspectives? Why does one see life and growth and rebirth while the other sees death and gloom?

Perhaps if we could peer inside the soul of these two we could gain a better insight into their perspectives.

Below are some close up images of the two souls

Close up of Soul One - Front

Close up of Soul One - Back

Rogue Art Genesis

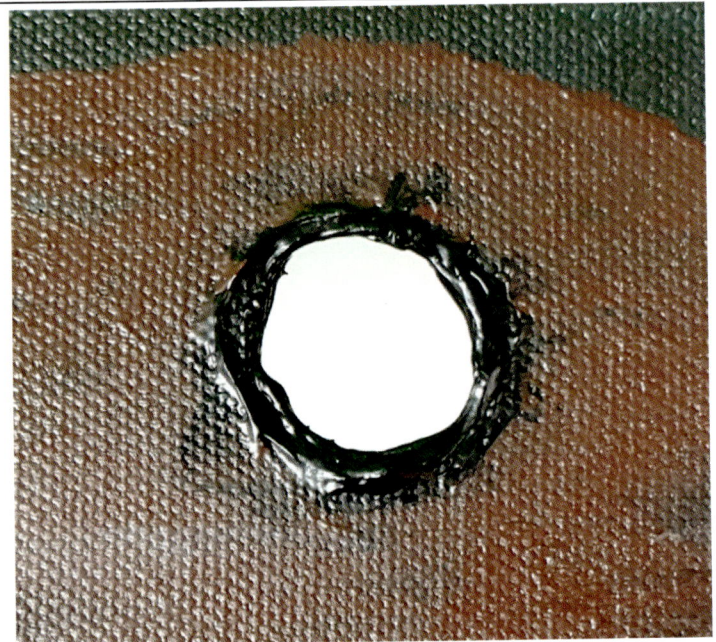

Close up of Soul Two - Front

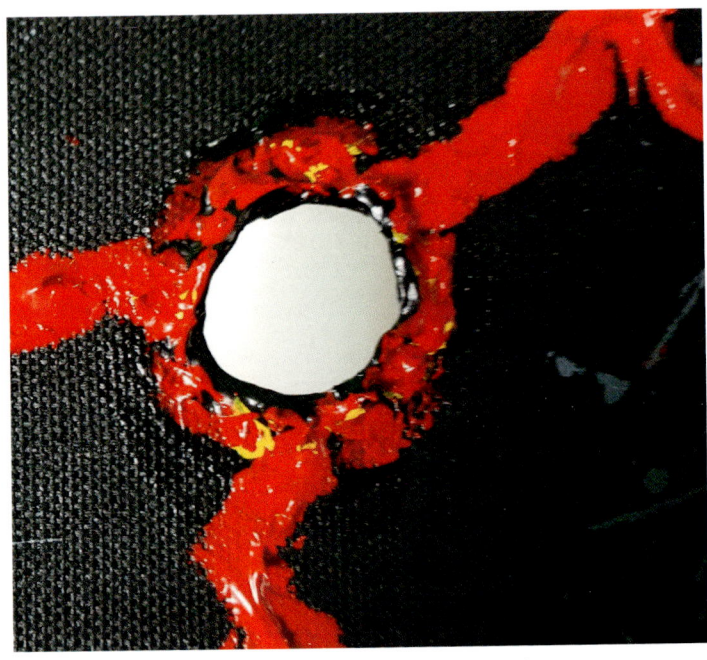

Close up of Soul Two - Back

Two Souls

(comments for viewing the back)

For man looks at the outward appearance, but Yahweh looks at the heart.

1 Samuel 16:7b (World English Bible)

Consider the two souls from the inside.

One is centered in light emanating a rainbow representing the full gamut of healthy human emotion.

The other is a soul in chaos; random splatters of thought and emotion tossed about his dark canvas. The soul is wounded with an injury so severe it is visible from the outside. Veins of infectious thoughts seep from the opening until the whole of his reality is defined by the wound.

Questions to Consider

What does the wound represent?

Why has it overtaken the soul?

Notice the soul centered in light has a wound as well and it is as large and significant as the soul in chaos. Yet he appears to not be consumed by the wound. Why?

Look closely at the wound of the soul in light. It is surrounded by hands representing the healing presence of people committed to bringing restoration to the wounded.

Most of the healing hands appear wounded in some fashion. What is the significance of this?

The hands appear to be painted by children. What is the significance?

How long has it been since these two souls experienced their wounds?

How long did it take for the soul in chaos to be consumed by the wound? How long did it take for the soul in light to be healed?

Did the soul in light submit himself to the hands of the healers, or did the healers take the initiative?

Where are the hands of the healers for the soul in chaos? How long will he bear the pain of his wound alone?

Call to Action

Although these two souls represent two extremes which one do you more readily relate to?
    Are you wounded?
    Are you healed?
    Can you be an instrument of healing?

If you are wounded, are you carrying the burden alone? If so, how might you open yourself up to people who can be agents of restoration?

Do you know someone who is wounded? Will you be an agent of healing to them? How might this look if you took this notion from the abstract to the practical? What practical steps could you take to bring the beginnings of healing (remembering that healing does not typically come from one large event, but rather many small steps delivered consistently and lovingly over time)?

Final Thoughts

The Prayer of St. Francis of Assisi

Lord, make me an instrument of Your peace;
Where there is hatred, let me sow love;
Where there is injury, pardon;
Where there is discord, harmony;
Where there is error, truth;
Where there is doubt, faith;
Where there is despair, hope;
Where there is darkness, light;
And where there is sadness, joy.

O Divine Master, Grant that I may not so much seek
To be consoled as to console;
To be understood as to understand;
To be loved as to love.
For it is in giving that we receive;
It is in pardoning that we are pardoned;
And it is in dying that we are born to eternal life.

Chapter 12: The Three Mirrors

Mirror of Our Present Reality

Mirror of Our Fondest Hopes

Mirror of God's Earnest Longing for Us

God said, "Let us make man in our image, after our likeness
                                         Genesis 1:26a (World English Bible)

Introduction

Consider for a moment the three distinct mirrors above. In your mind let each mirror reflect different aspects of yourself as defined below.

Mirror of Our Present Reality

As you look at the first mirror let it represent the mirror that reflects the way you currently see yourself and your present reality. Notice there are several spots that do not reflect. What do these "blind spots" represent to you? Why are there blind spots? Can perhaps others see these things that you are blind to?

Mirror of Our Fondest Hopes

Let the second mirror represent the reflection of how you wish your life to be. Let the light reflecting through the rainbow of colors be a metaphor for your many hopes surrounding your life. What is your fondest hope for your life? If this mirror actually worked and showed reflections of your most sincere desires, what would it reveal?

Mirror of God's Earnest Longing for Us

Let the third mirror represent the reflection of God's earnest desires for our lives. Notice that light seems to be emanating from the mirror. What might this light represent? If this mirror actually worked and genuinely displayed God's earnest longing for your life, what would the reflection look like?

Questions to Consider

Are the reflections from these three mirrors different? Why? Do they need to be? Or could your dreams, God's dreams, and your actual real life experience be one and the same? As we look deeply into the three mirrors and see God's dream for your life, your dream for your life and your current reality, is there anything keeping these three reflections from revealing the same image?

Is there a difference between the hopes you have for your life and God's hope for your life? If there is a difference and you could only choose one of these hopes to live out, which do you suppose would bring you more joy? Which would allow you to sense you were living the purpose of your creation?

Is there a difference between your current reality and your dreams for your life? Is there a difference between your current reality and God's dreams for you? If so, why?

Call to Action

As you consider if there are any differences between the three reflections of God's earnest longing for you, your dreams and your present reality, what comes to mind? What practical action can you take so that these three images become more closely aligned? What steps will you take to have your dreams more connected with God's dreams for you? If you are not living into your hopes, what practical steps can you take to move closer to living out your dreams? Pick something you can do today to more closely align the reflections of the three mirrors and then do it.

Final Thoughts

Be Thou My Vision

Words attributed to Dallan Forgaill, 6th century; translated from ancient Irish to English by Mary E. Byrne in 1905, and versed by Eleanor H. Hull, 1912.

> Be Thou my vision, O Lord of my heart;
> Naught be all else to me, save that Thou art.
> Thou my best thought, by day or by night,
> Waking or sleeping, Thy presence my light.
>
> Be Thou my wisdom, and Thou my true word;
> I ever with Thee and Thou with me, Lord;
> Thou my great Father, I Thy true son;
> Thou in me dwelling, and I with Thee one.
>
> Be Thou my battle shield, sword for the fight;
> Be Thou my dignity, Thou my delight;
> Thou my soul's shelter, Thou my high tower:
> Raise Thou me heavenward, O power of my power.
>
> Riches I heed not, nor man's empty praise,
> Thou mine inheritance, now and always:
> Thou and Thou only, first in my heart,
> High King of Heaven, my treasure Thou art.
>
> High King of Heaven, my victory won,
> May I reach Heaven's joys, O bright Heaven's sun!
> Heart of my own heart, whatever befall,
> Still be my vision, O ruler of all.

Conclusion

Art is emotion. I trust that you could feel the art at work within you. As you mused over the meaning of the works and allowed them to soak into you like a gentle rain onto fine soil, I trust the paint came alive for you in practical ways.

So the question is; what will you do now? Perhaps you will pursue more fervently one of the calls to action. Maybe you will get a group of friends together to intently consider how to live more fully into the enlightenment you gained. Possibly you will create new works of Rogue Art or invent a new art form altogether.

Whatever the case may be, I hope that you are more fully alive than when you started this journey and that you continue this growth into ever transforming light. As a garden flourishes from light and rain, may your journey into Rogue Art bring you ongoing life and light.

Sincerely,

Brad